Holiday Cocktails

The possibilities for cocktails are endless. They can be new or traditional, with or without alcohol, based on spirits, wines, fruit juices or teas. The only thing they all have in common is that they are temptingly, blissfully, and absolutely delicious.

Holiday Cocktails

Gabrielle Mander

Contents

NOTE
In this book the measure for drinks has been rounded
up to 1 fl oz; if you do not have a drinks measure, use 2
tablespoons. All drinks recipes serve 1 unless otherwise
stated. Standard level spoon measures are used in all
recipes.

Introduction

Everyone loves a party! What better way to say "hello" to old friends, "welcome" to your new neighbors, or celebrate a festive occasion? A party can be two friends enjoying a cocktail or a gathering of the clans. In these pages there are delicious concoctions of spirits and wines in celebration punches, scrumptious alcohol- free cups based on fruit juices, teas and herbs, and cocktails, classic and new, with or without alcohol, that make every party one to remember!

History

Who invented the cocktail? This must be one of the ten questions in the world to which everyone is sure they have the definitive answer and no two will be the same!

Some people quote the wonderful story of the Mexican princess Xoctl, who served a delicious drink to American officers at her father's court. In a classic misunderstanding, the officers misheard and thought that Xoctl was the name of the drink rather than the princess and passed the name cocktail into the history of the bar.

The creative and imaginative names which many of the modern concoctions bear are said to have originated during the Prohibition in the USA, when furtive drinkers in the speakeasies were able to fool the vigilant authorities into believing that the tipples they sipped in tea-cups and saucers were innocent of bootleg alcohol, by using a code of fanciful names. In any event, the exciting names lend glamor and humor to the whole exercise of making and serving cocktails. It is obvious that they are meant to be fun!

They are also intended to be made individually, to the drinker's taste, which is why most cocktail recipes serve one. The individual drink was developed from the much earlier punches and cups which had always been served at public entertainments, private parties and dances. The cocktail hour, before dinner, is enjoying a great revival, representing that time between the rigors of the day and a relaxed evening. Entertaining friends at home has never been easier, and new cocktails and punches are being invented all the time. Why not create your own, and add your name to cocktail history?

and culture

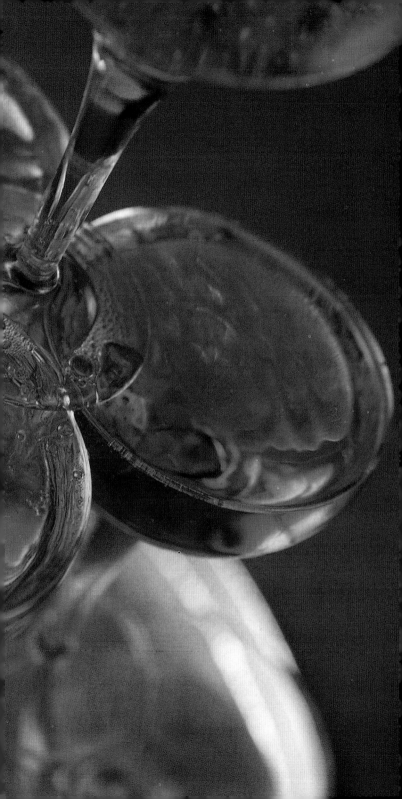

Party planning

What is the secret of a truly successful party? Great music? Good conversation? Soft lighting? Although all of these play a part, the secret ingredient that ensures a successful party is forward planning.

It is most important that you are relaxed and confident when you greet your guests. Planning means thinking about how many people you can entertain comfortably. It doesn't matter whether you issue your invitations by post, phone, fax or e-mail or even face-to-face, as long as you are quite clear about the kind of party you are giving. Let your guests know when they are expected, and what to expect from you – drinks or drinks and food, a casual party or something more formal.

Decorating drinks

Some cocktails and drinks have traditional, almost ritual decoration – an olive in a dry martini, for example, or a sugar-rimmed glass for a mint julep.

Tequila-based cocktails are usually served in a glass that is rimmed with salt. The principle of rimming the glass is the same for both salt and sugar. Rub a piece of citrus fruit around the top of the glass, then dip the moist rim into a saucer of salt or sugar.

Decorations should always be appropriate to the drink. Spirals of lemon or orange zest cut from the fruit in one piece take practice. Umbrellas and swizzle sticks are optional extras, and many drinks are served with straws.

Glasses

Using ordinary wine glasses, you can serve cocktails and punches with impunity!

A couple of brandy balloons, some tall glasses for highballs and some short, straight-sided tumblers for drinks served over ice, such as Bloody Marys, will satisfy even the fussiest connoisseur. Champagne flutes are useful and cleverly designed to keep the bubbles in the glass, with a stem that stops the drink being warmed by the drinker's hand. Add an ice bucket, a cocktail shaker or screw-topped jar and a lemon squeezer – and you are fully equipped.

If you do not have time to prepare snacks for your guests, scatter a few bowls around the room containing a selection of stylish nibbles, such as olives and chilies, mixed dried fruits, pistachios and cashews.

Estimating quantities

When planning a drinks party, it is difficult to estimate how many bottles of wine and spirits to order. This will depend on the occasion, the size of the glasses and the thirst of your guests, but a rough guide to quantities is as follows:

In single measures for cocktails, spirits and vermouths give just over 30 drinks a bottle. You will get 16–20 drinks when mixing with soda, tonic, etc.

An average bottle of wine will yield 5–6 glasses, and Champagne 6–8 glasses. A 1 pint carton of fruit or tomato juice will give 4–6 drinks.

You should be ready to offer 3–5 drinks per person.

Basic recipes

Sugar syrup

4 tablespoons sugar
4 tablespoons water

Put the sugar and water in a small
saucepan, bring slowly to the boil,
stirring to dissolve the sugar.
Boil the mixture without stirring for
1–2 minutes.
Pour into a sterilized bottle, seal and
refrigerate for up to two months.

Mint syrup

handful of fresh mint
3 cups sugar
8 fl oz water

Crush the mint, dissolve the sugar in the water
and add the mint to it. Boil for 5 minutes.
Leave to stand until cool. Strain into a sterilized
bottle and cork tightly. The syrup will keep in a
refrigerator for up to 2 months.
Makes about 1¼ cups

Roman Punch

4 cups sugar
juice of 3 oranges
juice of 10 lemons
2 pints Champagne
 or sparkling wine
2 pints dark rum
½ fl oz orange bitters
grated zest of 1 orange
10 egg whites, beaten
orange slices, to decorate

Put the sugar into a large, chilled punch bowl and pour in the orange and lemon juices. Stir gently until the sugar has dissolved.

Add the Champagne or sparkling wine, rum, orange bitters, orange zest and the egg whites. Add plenty of ice cubes and stir well. Keep the bowl packed with ice to keep the punch chilled.

Decorate with orange slices before serving.

Serves 15–20

Christmas Punch

juice of 15 lemons
juice of 4 oranges
2½ cups sugar
½ pint orange curaçao
2 fl oz grenadine
2 fl oz brandy
4 pints sparkling mineral water
slices of orange and lemon, to decorate

Pour the lemon and orange juices into a jug.
Add the sugar and stir gently until it has
dissolved.
Place a large quantity of ice cubes in a large
punch bowl.
Add the fruit juices, orange curaçao, grenadine,
brandy and mineral water, and stir well.
Decorate with the slices of orange and lemon
before serving.
Serves 15–20

Champagne Punch

1 cup sugar

4 pints Champagne

2 pints sparkling mineral water

2 fl oz brandy

2 fl oz maraschino

2 fl oz orange curaçao

slices of seasonal fresh fruit, to decorate

Put plenty of ice cubes into a large punch bowl and add the sugar.

Pour in the Champagne, and stir gently until the sugar has dissolved.

Add the mineral water, brandy, maraschino and orange curaçao, and stir well.

Decorate with the sliced fruit and keep the bowl well chilled.

Serves 15–20

Cider Cup

1 fl oz maraschino
1 fl oz orange curaçao
1 fl oz brandy
2 pints medium-dry cider
slices of seasonal fruit, to decorate

Pour the maraschino, orange curaçao, brandy and cider into a large chilled bowl or jug. Add plenty of ice and stir gently. Decorate with slices of seasonal fruit and serve.
Serves 4–6

Pinot Noir Cup

1 cup sugar
6 pints Pinot Noir
4 pints sparkling mineral water
½ pint lemon juice
2 fl oz orange curaçao

Put the sugar into a large punch bowl containing plenty of ice. Pour in the Pinot Noir, mineral water, lemon juice and orange curaçao, and stir gently until the sugar is dissolved. Keep the punch bowl packed with ice.
Serves 20–25

Mulled White Wine

juice and finely grated zest of 1 lemon
4 tablespoons clear honey
1 x 2-inch cinnamon stick
1 bottle medium-dry white wine
4 tablespoons whisky
slices of orange, to decorate

Put the lemon juice and honey into a pan, and
stir gently. Add the lemon zest, cinnamon and
wine, and simmer gently for 10 minutes.
Remove the cinnamon stick.
Add the whisky and orange slices, and serve in
warmed glasses or mugs.
Serves 6

Glühwein

1 lemon
8 cloves
1 bottle red wine
½ cup sugar
2 x 2-inch cinnamon sticks
2 cups brandy

Spike the lemon with the cloves.
Put the lemon, red wine, sugar and cinnamon
sticks into a pan and heat to just below
simmering point for 10 minutes.

Reduce the heat and add the brandy. Warm gently for 2–3 minutes. Remove the lemon. Strain the liquid and serve immediately in warmed glasses or mugs.

Serves 6

Glögg

½ cup sugar
1 bottle brandy
12 cloves
pinch of ground cinnamon
pinch of grated nutmeg
¼ cup large raisins
¼ cup unsalted blanched almonds
4 cups medium sweet sherry

Put the sugar in a pan. Pour in the brandy and stir gently until the sugar is dissolved.
Add the cloves, cinnamon, nutmeg, raisins and almonds, and heat to just below simmering point for 10 minutes.
Heat the sherry separately to just below simmering point.
Ignite the spicy brandy mixture and pour in the hot sherry.
Serve immediately in warmed glasses or mugs.

Serves 8–10

Prohibition Punch

4 fl oz sugar syrup (see page 19)
2 cups lemon juice
4 cups apple juice
10 cups ginger ale
slices of orange and lemon,
    to decorate

Freeze 1 pint of water in a shallow container. Mix the sugar syrup and juices in a large chilled punch bowl. Add the ice, pour over the ginger ale, and decorate.
Serves 25–30

Jamaican Punch

3¾ cups ginger ale
2 cups cola
3¾ cups lemonade (fresh)
10 dashes of Angostura bitters
slices of lemon, to decorate

Freeze 1 pint of water in a shallow container. Put the ice into a chilled punch bowl and pour over the ginger ale, cola, lemonade and Angostura bitters and stir. Decorate with slices of lemon.
Serves 20

Lemonale

3½ pints strong tea, cooled
juice of 6 lemons
6 tablespoons sugar
4 cups ginger ale
sprigs of fresh mint and slices of lemon,
  to decorate

Freeze 1 pint of water in a shallow container.
Pour the tea into a large bowl or jug. Add the
lemon juice, sugar and ice. Stir until the sugar
is dissolved. Just before serving, pour in the
ginger ale and decorate.
Serves 20

Angel Punch

4 fl oz sugar syrup (see page 19)
3¾ cups green or black tea, cooled
1½ cups lemon juice
3 pints white grape juice
3 pints soda water

Freeze 1 pint of water in a shallow container.
Stir the sugar syrup, tea and fruit juices in a
jug, and chill. Put the ice and punch in a large
punch bowl. Stir in the soda water and serve.
Serves 20

California Dreaming

2 dashes of Kirsch
3 fl oz pineapple juice
dash of lemon juice
Champagne, to top up
slices of pineapple, to decorate

Crush some ice cubes and put into a cocktail shaker. Pour in the Kirsch and juices, and shake for 45 seconds. Pour into a glass and top up with Champagne. Decorate with pineapple.
Makes 1

Americana

½ teaspoon sugar
1 fl oz Bourbon whisky
dash of Angostura bitters
Champagne, to top up
a slice of peach, to decorate

Dissolve the sugar in the Bourbon in a wide Champagne glass. Stir in the Angostura bitters. Top up the glass with Champagne and decorate with a peach slice.
Makes 1

Honeydew

1 fl oz gin
½ fl oz lemon juice
dash of Pernod
Champagne, to top up
¼ cup Honeydew melon, diced,
    to decorate

Put the gin, lemon juice and Pernod into a
blender with some ice. Blend for 30 seconds.
Pour into a large glass. Top up with
Champagne and decorate with the melon.
Makes 1

Chicago

1 fl oz brandy
dash of curaçao
pinch of sugar
2 dashes of Angostura bitters
sugar and lemon juice, to frost
Champagne, to top up

Pour the brandy, curaçao, sugar and bitters into
a cocktail shaker with some ice. Shake well for
30 seconds.
Sugar frost a glass with lemon. Strain into a
brandy glass and top up with Champagne.
Makes 1

Caribbean Champagne

¼ fl oz light rum
¼ fl oz crème de banane
dash of Angostura bitters
chilled Champagne or sparkling dry
   white wine, to top up
TO DECORATE
1 slice of banana
1 slice of pineapple
cocktail cherries

Pour the rum, crème de banane and Angostura bitters into a Champagne glass.

Top up with Champagne or sparkling white wine, and stir gently.

Decorate with a slice of banana, pineapple and cherries, all speared on a cocktail stick.

Makes 1

Kir Royale

1 teaspoon crème de cassis
5–6 fl oz chilled Champagne
  or sparkling dry white wine

Measure the crème de cassis into a chilled tall
glass or Champagne flute.
Pour in the chilled Champagne or sparkling dry
white wine, and stir until just blended.
Makes 1

Bellini

2 fl oz unsweetened peach juice,
  (preferably fresh)
4 fl oz chilled Champagne or sparkling
  dry white wine
dash of grenadine (optional)

Measure the peach juice into a large wine glass
and stir in the chilled Champagne or sparkling
dry white wine.
Add the grenadine, if using, and stir gently.
Makes 1

Bloody Mary

1 fl oz vodka
4 fl oz tomato juice
2 dashes of Worcestershire sauce
a good squeeze of lemon juice
dash of Tabasco sauce
salt and pepper to taste
slice of lemon, sprig of mint or stick of
  celery, to decorate

Shake all the ingredients together with ice and
strain into a tumbler or balloon wine glass. Add
your chosen decoration.
Makes 1

Variations
Bloody Maria is a version made with tequila
instead of vodka.
Virgin Mary omits the vodka.

Black Russian

2 fl oz vodka
1 fl oz Kahlúa

Put some ice cubes into a whisky tumbler and pour over the vodka and Kahlúa.
To make a White Russian, top up with heavy cream, and to make a longer drink, use a tall tumbler and top up with a cola.
Makes 1

Muddy River

1 fl oz vodka
1½ fl oz dark crème de cacao
1 fl oz Kahlúa
3 fl oz cream

Half-fill a tumbler with ice cubes.
Pour the vodka, crème de cacao, Kahlúa and cream into a cocktail shaker. Shake for about 30 seconds, then pour over the ice and serve.
Makes 1

Coffee Egg Nog

1½ fl oz whisky

1 fl oz Kahlúa

2 teaspoons heavy cream

1½ teaspoons sugar syrup (see page 19)

1 egg, beaten

½ teaspoon instant coffee

4 fl oz milk

1 teaspoon coriander, very finely chopped.

Half-fill a cocktail shaker with ice cubes.
Pour the whisky, Kahlúa, cream and sugar
syrup into the shaker.

Add the egg, instant coffee and milk and shake
well for about 45 seconds.

Half-fill a tall glass with ice. Strain the mixture
over the ice and stir gently.

Dust with coriander and serve.

Makes 1

Harvey Wallbanger

1½ fl oz vodka
4 fl oz orange juice
2–3 teaspoons Galliano

Half-fill a cocktail shaker with ice and pour in
the vodka and orange juice. Shake for about
30 seconds, then strain into a long glass almost
filled with ice cubes.
Float the Galliano on top. Serve with a straw.
Makes 1

Long Island Iced Tea

½ fl oz gin
½ fl oz vodka
½ fl oz white rum
½ fl oz tequila
½ fl oz triple sec (e.g. Cointreau)
1 fl oz lemon juice
½ teaspoon sugar syrup (see page 19)
cola, to top up
lemon slices and mint sprigs, to decorate

Stir the first 7 ingredients with ice, then strain
into a long glass almost filled with ice cubes.
Top up with cola and decorate with lemon
slices and mint sprigs.
Makes 1

Dry Martini

2 fl oz London Dry gin
½ fl oz dry vermouth
a green olive or a thin strip of
lemon zest, to decorate

Pour the gin and vermouth over ice in a mixing
glass, stir well, then strain into a chilled cocktail
glass. Either decorate with a green olive, or
squeeze and twist the lemon peel over the
glass, then drop it in.
Makes 1

Strawberry Daiquiri

1 fl oz white rum
½ fl oz crème de fraises
½ fl oz fresh lemon juice
4 ripe strawberries, hulled
2 scoops of crushed ice
strawberries, to decorate

Place all the ingredients in a blender and blend
at slow speed for 5 seconds, then at high speed
for about 20 seconds. Pour into a chilled sour
glass, decorate with the fruit and serve with
straws.
Makes 1

Egg Nog

1 egg
1 tablespoon sugar
2 fl oz brandy
2 fl oz milk
little grated nutmeg, to decorate

Half-fill a cocktail shaker with ice. Add the egg,
sugar, brandy and milk, and shake well for
about 60 seconds.
Strain into a tall tumbler and sprinkle a little
grated nutmeg on top.
Makes 1

Kahlúa Sour

1½ fl oz Kahlúa
1 fl oz lemon juice
½ teaspoon sugar
TO DECORATE
maraschino cherry
slice of lemon

Pour the Kahlúa and lemon juice into a cocktail
shaker.
Add the sugar and shake for about 45 seconds.
Pour into a tumbler and decorate with a
maraschino cherry and a slice of lemon.
Makes 1

Tom Collins

1½ teaspoons sugar
juice of ½ lemon
2 fl oz gin
soda water, to top up
slice of lemon and maraschino
   cherry, to decorate (optional)

Half-fill a cocktail shaker with ice. Add the sugar,
lemon juice, and gin and shake well. Strain into
a glass, and top up with ice and soda water.
Decorate with a slice of lemon and a cherry,
if liked.
Makes 1

Thin Mint

1 egg yolk
1 teaspoon dark chocolate, grated
2 fl oz peppermint Schnapps
½ fl oz brandy
chocolate matchsticks, to decorate

Put the egg yolk into a cocktail shaker and
sprinkle in the grated chocolate. Add the
peppermint Schnapps and the brandy, and
shake well. Strain the cocktail into a glass and
serve with chocolate matchsticks.
Makes 1

Rum Collins

juice of 1 lime
1 teaspoon sugar
2 fl oz dark rum
soda water, to top up
slice of lemon and maraschino cherry,
    to decorate

Half-fill a cocktail shaker with ice. Add the lime
juice, stir in the sugar and rum, and shake well.
Strain into a tall glass, add more ice and top up
with soda water. Decorate with a slice of lemon
and a cherry.
Makes 1

Grenade

4 fl oz lemon juice
2 teaspoons grenadine
2 egg yolks
zest of 2 lemons, cut in spirals,
to decorate

Half-fill a cocktail shaker with some
ice cubes.
Add the lemon juice, grenadine and
the egg yolks.
Shake well for about 45 seconds.
Strain into cocktail glasses and dangle
the spirals of lemon rind over the edge
of the glasses.
Decorate with paper parasols, if liked,
and serve.
Makes 2

Sunset Surf

3 tablespoons redcurrant jelly
6 tablespoons vanilla ice cream
1 pint soda water
maraschino cherries or redcurrants,
  to decorate

Place the redcurrant jelly, vanilla ice cream and
1¼ cups of soda water in a blender and blend
at slow speed for 5 seconds, then at high speed
for 20 seconds.
Pour into tall glasses and top up with the
remaining soda water.
Decorate with maraschino cherries or fresh
redcurrants, if available.
Makes 2

Mock Kir

1 bottle non-alcoholic white wine
2 tablespoons blackcurrant cordial

Put half a tablespoon of blackcurrant cordial in
each wine glass and top up with the chilled
white wine. Stir gently to combine.
Makes 4

Frosty Lime

1 scoop lime sorbet
4 teaspoons grapefruit juice
4 teaspoons mint syrup (see page 19)
sprig of fresh mint and slice of lemon,
**   to decorate**

Put the sorbet, grapefruit juice and mint syrup
into a blender and blend at high speed for
about 30 seconds. Strain into a Champagne
saucer or cocktail glass and decorate with fresh
mint. Cut a small slit in the lemon slice and fix
onto the rim of the glass.
Makes 1

Spiced Iced Coffee

1½ pints triple strength coffee
pared zest of half an orange
14 fl oz whipping cream
a little grated nutmeg
4 x 2-inch cinnamon sticks

After making the coffee, drop in the orange
rind and chill. Add cream to taste, and top
lightly with whipped cream. Sprinkle with the
grated nutmeg on top.
Use the cinnamon stick to stir.
Makes 4

Florentine Coffee

Add a drop of almond extract to a freshly made
cup of very strong (espresso) coffee. Drink it as
it is or serve with a cube of sugar, if you prefer.
Makes 1

Iced Apple Tea

1 oz tea leaves or 1 tea bag
3¼ cups cold water
3¼ cups apple juice
juice of 1 lemon
1 teaspoon sugar (optional)
8 slices of lemon or orange and
8 sprigs of fresh mint, to decorate

Put the tea and the water in a large jug and
leave to steep overnight and strain if necessary.
Add the apple juice, lemon and sugar to taste.
Add plenty of ice and garnish with the lemon
or orange slices and sprigs of mint. Pour into
tall tumblers or tea glasses and serve.

Makes 6–8

Index

First published in the UK in 1997 by Hamlyn, an imprint of Reed
International Books Limited.
This US edition copyright © 1997 Reed International Books Limited.
Printed in China.

Photography by Jean Cazals